Tracing Your Ancestry
LOGBOOK

F. WILBUR HELMBOLD

Oxmoor House, Inc.
Birmingham

ISBN: 0-8487-0414-2

Library of Congress Catalog Card Number: 76-14109

Manufactured in the United States of America

Tracing Your Ancestry Logbook

Editor: Karen Phillips Irons

Design: Bob Nance

ANCESTOR CHART NO. _____

Date _____

Name of compiler _____

Address _____

City _____ State _____

Person No. 1 on this chart is identical to person

No. _____ on chart No. _____

b   Date of birth
pb   Place of birth
m   Date of marriage
d   Date of death
pd   Place of death

Refer to name and number

Form 1

16 _____ (Father of No. 8) . Continued on chart _____

17 _____ (Mother of No. 8) Continued on chart _____

18 _____ (Father of No. 9) Continued on chart _____

19 _____ (Mother of No. 9) Continued on chart _____

20 _____ (Father of No. 10) Continued on chart _____

21 _____ (Mother of No. 10) Continued on chart _____

22 _____ (Father of No. 11) Continued on chart _____

23 _____ (Mother of No. 11) Continued on chart _____

24 _____ (Father of No. 12) Continued on chart _____

25 _____ (Mother of No. 12) Continued on chart _____

26 _____ (Father of No. 13) Continued on chart _____

27 _____ (Mother of No. 13) Continued on chart _____

28 _____ (Father of No. 14) Continued on chart _____

29 _____ (Mother of No. 14) Continued on chart _____

30 _____ (Father of No. 15) Continued on chart _____

31 _____ (Mother of No. 15) Continued on chart _____

8 _____ (Father of No. 4)
b
pb
m
d
pd

9 _____ (Mother of No. 4)
b
pb
d
pd

10 _____ (Father of No. 5)
b
pb
m
d
pd

11 _____ (Mother of No. 5)
b
pb
d
pd

12 _____ (Father of No. 6)
b
pb
m
d
pd

13 _____ (Mother of No. 6)
b
pb
d
pd

14 _____ (Father of No. 7)
b
pb
m
d
pd

15 _____ (Mother of No. 7)
b
pb
d
pd

4 _____ (Father of No. 2)
b
pb
m
d
pd

5 _____ (Mother of No. 2)
b
pb
d
pd

6 _____ (Father of No. 3)
b
pb
m
d
pd

7 _____ (Mother of No. 3)
b
pb
d
pd

2 _____ (Father of No. 1)
b
pb
m
d
pd

3 _____ (Mother of No. 1)
b
pb
d
pd

1 _____
b
pb
m
d
pd

ANCESTOR CHART NO. _____

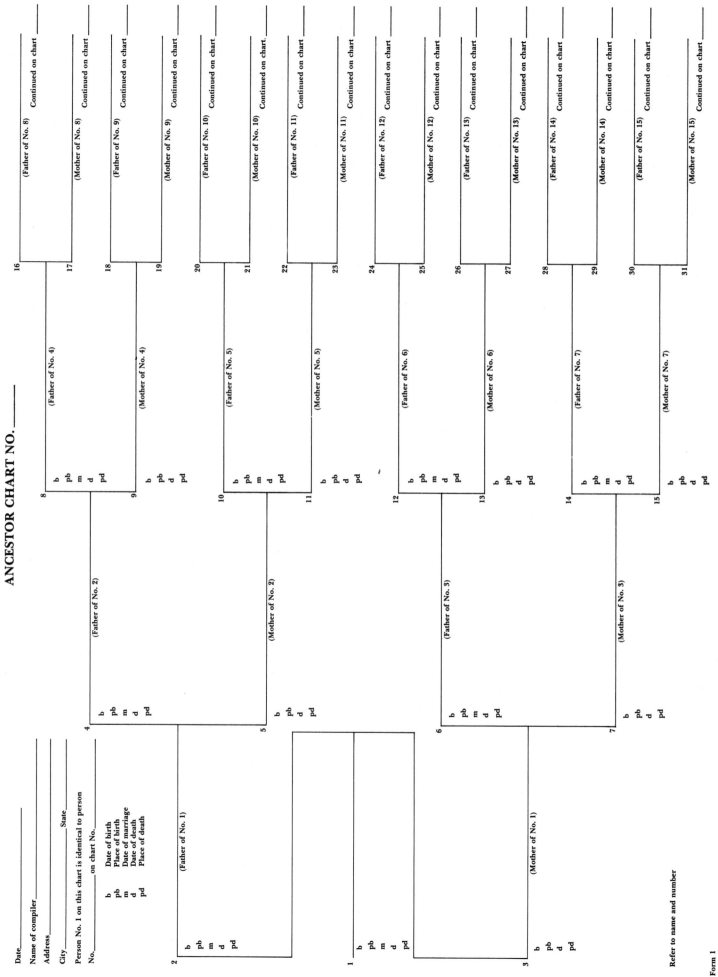

Date _____

Name of compiler _____

Address _____

City _____ State _____

Person No. 1 on this chart is identical to person

No. _____ on chart No. _____

b   Date of birth
pb   Place of birth
m   Date of marriage
d   Date of death
pd   Place of death

Refer to name and number

Form 1

1

2 (Father of No. 1)

b
pb
m
d
pd

3 (Mother of No. 1)

b
pb
d
pd

4 (Father of No. 2)

b
pb
m
d
pd

5 (Mother of No. 2)

b
pb
d
pd

6 (Father of No. 3)

b
pb
m
d
pd

7 (Mother of No. 3)

b
pb
d
pd

8 (Father of No. 4)

b
pb
m
d
pd

9 (Mother of No. 4)

b
pb
d
pd

10 (Father of No. 5)

b
pb
m
d
pd

11 (Mother of No. 5)

b
pb
d
pd

12 (Father of No. 6)

b
pb
m
d
pd

13 (Mother of No. 6)

b
pb
d
pd

14 (Father of No. 7)

b
pb
m
d
pd

15 (Mother of No. 7)

b
pb
d
pd

16 (Father of No. 8)   Continued on chart _____

17 (Mother of No. 8)   Continued on chart _____

18 (Father of No. 9)   Continued on chart _____

19 (Mother of No. 9)   Continued on chart _____

20 (Father of No. 10)   Continued on chart _____

21 (Mother of No. 10)   Continued on chart. _____

22 (Father of No. 11)   Continued on chart _____

23 (Mother of No. 11)   Continued on chart _____

24 (Father of No. 12)   Continued on chart _____

25 (Mother of No. 12)   Continued on chart _____

26 (Father of No. 13)   Continued on chart _____

27 (Mother of No. 13)   Continued on chart _____

28 (Father of No. 14)   Continued on chart _____

29 (Mother of No. 14)   Continued on chart _____

30 (Father of No. 15)   Continued on chart _____

31 (Mother of No. 15)   Continued on chart _____

ANCESTOR CHART NO._____

Date _____
Name of compiler _____
Address _____
City _____ State _____
Person No. 1 on this chart is identical to person
No. _____ on chart No. _____

b   Date of birth
pb   Place of birth
m   Date of marriage
d   Date of death
pd   Place of death

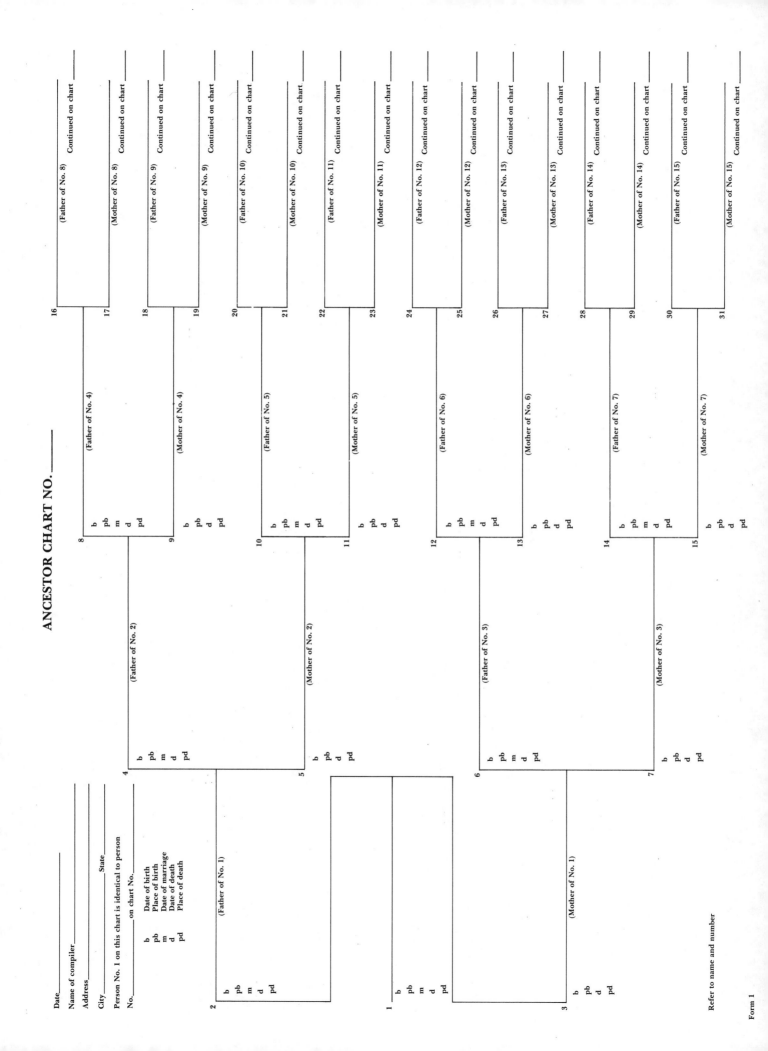

16 _____ (Father of No. 8) Continued on chart _____
17 _____ (Mother of No. 8) Continued on chart _____
18 _____ (Father of No. 9) Continued on chart _____
19 _____ (Mother of No. 9) Continued on chart _____
20 _____ (Father of No. 10) Continued on chart _____
21 _____ (Mother of No. 10) Continued on chart _____
22 _____ (Father of No. 11) Continued on chart _____
23 _____ (Mother of No. 11) Continued on chart _____
24 _____ (Father of No. 12) Continued on chart _____
25 _____ (Mother of No. 12) Continued on chart _____
26 _____ (Father of No. 13) Continued on chart _____
27 _____ (Mother of No. 13) Continued on chart _____
28 _____ (Father of No. 14) Continued on chart _____
29 _____ (Mother of No. 14) Continued on chart _____
30 _____ (Father of No. 15) Continued on chart _____
31 _____ (Mother of No. 15) Continued on chart _____

8 (Father of No. 4) b pb m d pd
9 (Mother of No. 4) b pb d pd
10 (Father of No. 5) b pb m d pd
11 (Mother of No. 5) b pb d pd
12 (Father of No. 6) b pb m d pd
13 (Mother of No. 6) b pb d pd
14 (Father of No. 7) b pb m d pd
15 (Mother of No. 7) b pb d pd

4 (Father of No. 2) b pb m d pd
5 (Mother of No. 2) b pb d pd
6 (Father of No. 3) b pb m d pd
7 (Mother of No. 3) b pb d pd

2 (Father of No. 1) b pb m d pd
3 (Mother of No. 1) b pb d pd

1 b pb m d pd

Refer to name and number

Form 1

ANCESTOR CHART NO. _____

Date _____
Name of compiler _____
Address _____
City _____ State _____
Person No. 1 on this chart is identical to person
No. _____ on chart No. _____

b   Date of birth
pb   Place of birth
m   Date of marriage
d   Date of death
pd   Place of death

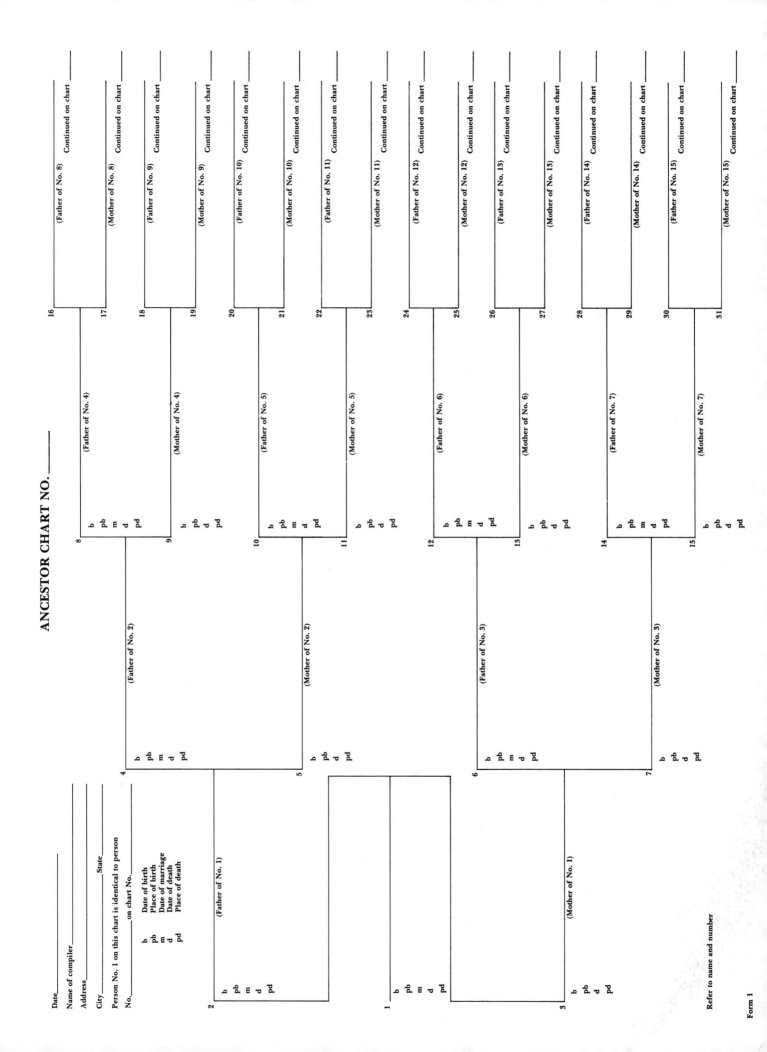

Refer to name and number

Form 1

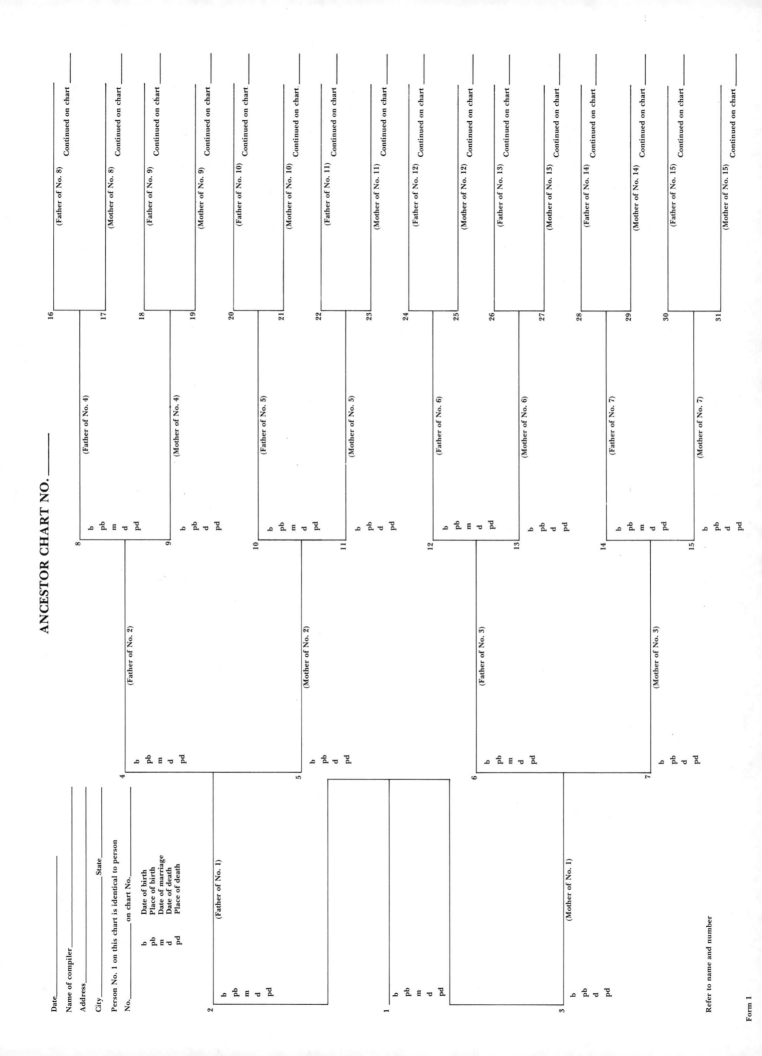

ANCESTOR CHART NO. _____

Date _____
Name of compiler _____
Address _____
City _____ State _____
Person No. 1 on this chart is identical to person
No. _____ on chart No. _____

b   Date of birth
pb   Place of birth
m   Date of marriage
d   Date of death
pd   Place of death

2 _____ (Father of No. 1)
b
pb
m
d
pd

1 _____
b
pb
m
d
pd

3 _____ (Mother of No. 1)
b
pb
d
pd

4 _____ (Father of No. 2)
b
pb
m
d
pd

5 _____ (Mother of No. 2)
b
pb
d
pd

6 _____ (Father of No. 3)
b
pb
m
d
pd

7 _____ (Mother of No. 3)
b
pb
d
pd

8 _____ (Father of No. 4)
b
pb
m
d
pd

9 _____ (Mother of No. 4)
b
pb
d
pd

10 _____ (Father of No. 5)
b
pb
m
d
pd

11 _____ (Mother of No. 5)
b
pb
d
pd

12 _____ (Father of No. 6)
b
pb
m
d
pd

13 _____ (Mother of No. 6)
b
pb
d
pd

14 _____ (Father of No. 7)
b
pb
m
d
pd

15 _____ (Mother of No. 7)
b
pb
d
pd

16 _____ (Father of No. 8)   Continued on chart _____
17 _____ (Mother of No. 8)   Continued on chart _____
18 _____ (Father of No. 9)   Continued on chart _____
19 _____ (Mother of No. 9)   Continued on chart _____
20 _____ (Father of No. 10)   Continued on chart _____
21 _____ (Mother of No. 10)   Continued on chart. _____
22 _____ (Father of No. 11)   Continued on chart _____
23 _____ (Mother of No. 11)   Continued on chart _____
24 _____ (Father of No. 12)   Continued on chart _____
25 _____ (Mother of No. 12)   Continued on chart _____
26 _____ (Father of No. 13)   Continued on chart _____
27 _____ (Mother of No. 13)   Continued on chart _____
28 _____ (Father of No. 14)   Continued on chart _____
29 _____ (Mother of No. 14)   Continued on chart _____
30 _____ (Father of No. 15)   Continued on chart _____
31 _____ (Mother of No. 15)   Continued on chart _____

Refer to name and number

Form 1

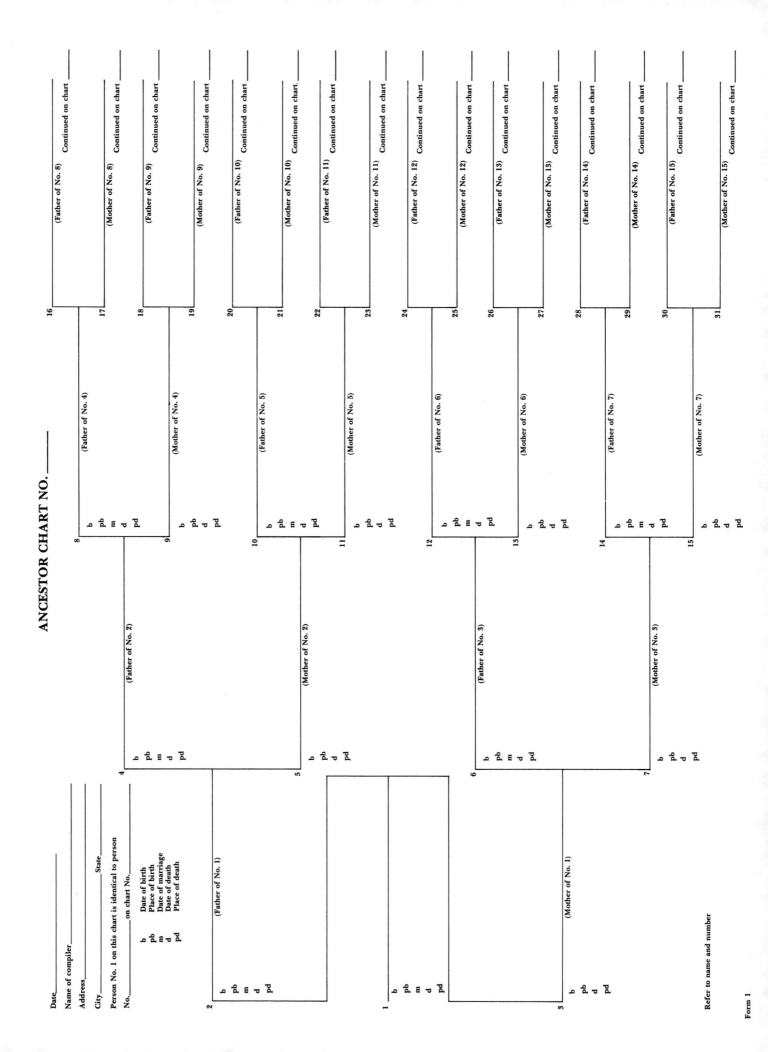

ANCESTOR CHART NO. _____

Date _____
Name of compiler _____
Address _____
City _____ State _____
Person No. 1 on this chart is identical to person
No. _____ on chart No. _____

b   Date of birth
pb   Place of birth
m   Date of marriage
d   Date of death
pd   Place of death

(Father of No. 1)

(Mother of No. 1)

1

2
b
pb
m
d
pd

(Father of No. 2)

3
b
pb
m
d
pd

(Mother of No. 2)

(Father of No. 3)

(Mother of No. 3)

4
b
pb
m
d
pd

(Father of No. 4)

5
b
pb
d
pd

(Mother of No. 4)

6
b
pb
m
d
pd

(Father of No. 5)

7
b
pb
m
d
pd

(Mother of No. 5)

(Father of No. 6)

(Mother of No. 6)

(Father of No. 7)

(Mother of No. 7)

8
b
pb
m
d
pd

(Father of No. 4)

9
b
pb
d
pd

(Mother of No. 4)

10
b
pb
m
d
pd

(Father of No. 5)

11
b
pb
d
pd

(Mother of No. 5)

12
b
pb
m
d
pd

(Father of No. 6)

13
b
pb
d
pd

(Mother of No. 6)

14
b
pb
m
d
pd

(Father of No. 7)

15
b
pb
d
pd

(Mother of No. 7)

16 _____ (Father of No. 8)   Continued on chart _____
17 _____ (Mother of No. 8)   Continued on chart _____
18 _____ (Father of No. 9)   Continued on chart _____
19 _____ (Mother of No. 9)   Continued on chart _____
20 _____ (Father of No. 10)   Continued on chart _____
21 _____ (Mother of No. 10)   Continued on chart _____
22 _____ (Father of No. 11)   Continued on chart _____
23 _____ (Mother of No. 11)   Continued on chart _____
24 _____ (Father of No. 12)   Continued on chart _____
25 _____ (Mother of No. 12)   Continued on chart _____
26 _____ (Father of No. 13)   Continued on chart _____
27 _____ (Mother of No. 13)   Continued on chart _____
28 _____ (Father of No. 14)   Continued on chart _____
29 _____ (Mother of No. 14)   Continued on chart _____
30 _____ (Father of No. 15)   Continued on chart _____
31 _____ (Mother of No. 15)   Continued on chart _____

Refer to name and number

Form 1

FAMILY GROUP RECORD

Wife			Husband	
		Name		
		Born		
		Married		
		Died		
		Burial		
		Father		
		Mother		
	husband	Other (if any)	wife	

Notes

Date married & spouse

#	Sex	Children in order of birth	Born Day Month Year	Where born	Died Day Month Year	Where died

Source	By

Form 2

FAMILY GROUP RECORD

Wife			Husband	
		Name		
		Born		
		Married		
		Died		
		Burial		
		Father		
		Mother		
husband		Other (if any)	wife	

Notes

Date married & spouse

#	Sex	Children in order of birth	Born Day Month Year	Where born	Died Day Month Year	Where died

Source	By

Form 2

FAMILY GROUP RECORD

Wife			Husband	
		Name		
		Born		
		Married		
		Died		
		Burial		
		Father		
		Mother		
husband		Other (if any)	wife	

Notes

Date married & spouse

#	Sex	Children in order of birth	Born Day Month Year	Where born	Died Day Month Year	Where died

Source	By

Form 2

FAMILY GROUP RECORD

Wife			Husband	
		Name		
		Born		
		Married		
		Died		
		Burial		
		Father		
		Mother		
	husband	Other (if any)	wife	

Notes

Date married & spouse

#	Sex	Children in order of birth	Born Day Month Year	Where born	Died Day Month Year	Where died

Source   By

Form 2

FAMILY GROUP RECORD

Wife			Husband	
		Name		
		Born		
		Married		
		Died		
		Burial		
		Father		
		Mother		
	husband	Other (if any)	wife	

Notes

Date married & spouse

#	Sex	Children in order of birth	Born Day Month Year	Where born	Died Day Month Year	Where died

Source

By

Form 2

FAMILY GROUP RECORD

	Wife			Husband	
		Name			
		Born			
		Married			
		Died			
		Burial			
		Father			
		Mother			
	husband	Other (if any)	wife		

Notes

Date married & spouse

#	Sex	Children in order of birth	Born Day Month Year	Where born	Died Day Month Year	Where died

Source   By

FAMILY GROUP RECORD

	Wife				Husband	
			Name			
			Born			
			Married			
			Died			
			Burial			
			Father			
			Mother			
		husband	Other (if any)	wife		

Notes

Date married & spouse

#	Sex	Children in order of birth	Born Day Month Year	Where born	Died Day Month Year	Where died

Source   By

FAMILY GROUP RECORD

	Wife			Husband	
		Name			
		Born			
		Married			
		Died			
		Burial			
		Father			
		Mother			
	husband	Other (if any)	wife		

Notes

Date married & spouse

#	Sex	Children in order of birth	Born Day Month Year	Where born	Died Day Month Year	Where died

Source _____ By _____

Form 2

FAMILY GROUP RECORD

	Wife			Husband	
			Name		
			Born		
			Married		
			Died		
			Burial		
			Father		
			Mother		
		husband	Other (if any)	wife	

Notes

Date married & spouse

#	Sex	Children in order of birth	Born Day Month Year	Where born	Died Day Month Year	Where died

Source　　　　　　　　　　　　　　　　By

Form 2

FAMILY GROUP RECORD

	Wife			Husband	
		Name			
		Born			
		Married			
		Died			
		Burial			
		Father			
		Mother			
	husband	Other (if any)	wife		

Notes

Date married & spouse

#	Sex	Children in order of birth	Born Day Month Year	Where born	Died Day Month Year	Where died

Source	By

Form 2

FAMILY GROUP RECORD

	Wife			Husband	
		Name			
		Born			
		Married			
		Died			
		Burial			
		Father			
		Mother			
	husband	Other (if any)	wife		

Notes

Date married & spouse

#	Sex	Children in order of birth	Born Day Month Year	Where born	Died Day Month Year	Where died

Source		By	

Form 2

FAMILY GROUP RECORD

	Wife			Husband
		Name		
		Born		
		Married		
		Died		
		Burial		
		Father		
		Mother		
	husband	Other (if any)	wife	

Notes

Date married & spouse

#	Sex	Children in order of birth	Born Day Month Year	Where born	Died Day Month Year	Where died

Source   By

Form 2

FAMILY GROUP RECORD

	Wife		Husband	
		Name		
		Born		
		Married		
		Died		
		Burial		
		Father		
		Mother		
husband		Other (if any)	wife	

Notes

Date married & spouse

#	Sex	Children in order of birth	Born Day Month Year	Where born	Died Day Month Year	Where died

Source _____ By _____

Form 2

FAMILY GROUP RECORD

	Wife			Husband	
		Name			
		Born			
		Married			
		Died			
		Burial			
		Father			
		Mother			
	husband	Other (if any)	wife		

Notes

Date married & spouse

#	Sex	Children in order of birth	Born Day Month Year	Where born	Died Day Month Year	Where died

Source   By

Form 2

FAMILY GROUP RECORD

	Wife			Husband	
		Name			
		Born			
		Married			
		Died			
		Burial			
		Father			
		Mother			
	husband	Other (if any)	wife		

Notes

Date married & spouse

#	Sex	Children in order of birth	Born Day Month Year	Where born	Died Day Month Year	Where died

Source   By

Form 2

FAMILY GROUP RECORD

	Wife		Husband
Name			
Born			
Married			
Died			
Burial			
Father			
Mother			
Other (if any)	husband		wife

Notes

Date married & spouse

#	Sex	Children in order of birth	Born Day Month Year	Where born	Died Day Month Year	Where died

Source		By	

FAMILY GROUP RECORD

	Wife			Husband
		Name		
		Born		
		Married		
		Died		
		Burial		
		Father		
		Mother		
	husband	Other (if any)	wife	

Notes

Date married & spouse

#	Sex	Children in order of birth	Born Day Month Year	Where born	Died Day Month Year	Where died

Source	By

Form 2

FAMILY GROUP RECORD

	Wife			Husband	
			Name		
			Born		
			Married		
			Died		
			Burial		
			Father		
			Mother		
	husband		Other (if any)	wife	

Notes

Date married & spouse

#	Sex	Children in order of birth	Born Day Month Year	Where born	Died Day Month Year	Where died

Source	By

FAMILY GROUP RECORD

	Wife		Husband	
		Name		
		Born		
		Married		
		Died		
		Burial		
		Father		
		Mother		
husband		Other (if any)	wife	

Notes

Date married & spouse

#	Sex	Children in order of birth	Born Day Month Year	Where born	Died Day Month Year	Where died

Source	By	

Form 2

FAMILY GROUP RECORD

	Wife			Husband	
			Name		
			Born		
			Married		
			Died		
			Burial		
			Father		
			Mother		
	husband	Other (if any)	wife		

Notes

Date married & spouse

#	Sex	Children in order of birth	Born Day Month Year	Where born	Died Day Month Year	Where died

Source

By

Form 2

FAMILY GROUP RECORD

	Wife			Husband	
			Name		
			Born		
			Married		
			Died		
			Burial		
			Father		
			Mother		
		husband	Other (if any)	wife	

Notes

Date married & spouse

#	Sex	Children in order of birth	Born Day Month Year	Where born	Died Day Month Year	Where died

Source		By	

Form 2

FAMILY GROUP RECORD

	Wife			Husband	
		Name			
		Born			
		Married			
		Died			
		Burial			
		Father			
		Mother			
	husband	Other (if any)	wife		

Notes

Date married & spouse

#	Sex	Children in order of birth	Born Day Month Year	Where born	Died Day Month Year	Where died

Source   By

Form 2

FAMILY GROUP RECORD

	Wife			Husband	
		Name			
		Born			
		Married			
		Died			
		Burial			
		Father			
		Mother			
	husband	Other (if any)	wife		

Notes

Date married & spouse

#	Sex	Children in order of birth	Born Day Month Year	Where born	Died Day Month Year	Where died

Source		By

Form 2

FAMILY GROUP RECORD

	Wife			Husband	
		Name			
		Born			
		Married			
		Died			
		Burial			
		Father			
		Mother			
	husband	Other (if any)	wife		

Notes

Date married & spouse

#	Sex	Children in order of birth	Born Day Month Year	Where born	Died Day Month Year	Where died

Source	By

Form 2

FAMILY GROUP RECORD

	Wife		Husband	
		Name		
		Born		
		Married		
		Died		
		Burial		
		Father		
		Mother		
	husband	Other (if any)	wife	

Notes

Date married & spouse

#	Sex	Children in order of birth	Born Day Month Year	Where born	Died Day Month Year	Where died

Source	By

Form 2

FAMILY GROUP RECORD

	Wife			Husband	
		Name			
		Born			
		Married			
		Died			
		Burial			
		Father			
		Mother			
	husband	Other (if any)	wife		

Notes

Date married & spouse

#	Sex	Children in order of birth	Born Day Month Year	Where born	Died Day Month Year	Where died

Source   By

Form 2

FAMILY GROUP RECORD

	Wife			Husband
		Name		
		Born		
		Married		
		Died		
		Burial		
		Father		
		Mother		
	husband	Other (if any)	wife	

Notes

Date married & spouse

#	Sex	Children in order of birth	Born Day Month Year	Where born	Died Day Month Year	Where died

Source   By

FAMILY GROUP RECORD

	Wife			Husband	
			Name		
			Born		
			Married		
			Died		
			Burial		
			Father		
			Mother		
	husband		Other (if any)	wife	

Notes

Date married & spouse

#	Sex	Children in order of birth	Born Day Month Year	Where born	Died Day Month Year	Where died

Source		By	

Form 2

FAMILY GROUP RECORD

	Wife				Husband	
			Name			
			Born			
			Married			
			Died			
			Burial			
			Father			
			Mother			
		husband	Other (if any)	wife		

Notes

Date married & spouse

#	Sex	Children in order of birth	Born Day Month Year	Where born	Died Day Month Year	Where died

Source   By

Form 2

FAMILY GROUP RECORD

	Wife			Husband	
		Name			
		Born			
		Married			
		Died			
		Burial			
		Father			
		Mother			
	husband	Other (if any)	wife		

Notes

Date married & spouse

#	Sex	Children in order of birth	Born Day Month Year	Where born	Died Day Month Year	Where died

Source _____ By _____

Form 2

FAMILY GROUP RECORD

	Wife			Husband	
		Name			
		Born			
		Married			
		Died			
		Burial			
		Father			
		Mother			
	husband	Other (if any)	wife		

Notes

Date married & spouse

#	Sex	Children in order of birth	Born Day Month Year	Where born	Died Day Month Year	Where died

Source _____ By _____

Form 2

FAMILY GROUP RECORD

	Wife			Husband	
			Name		
			Born		
			Married		
			Died		
			Burial		
			Father		
			Mother		
		husband	Other (if any)	wife	

Notes

Date married & spouse

#	Sex	Children in order of birth	Born Day Month Year	Where born	Died Day Month Year	Where died

Source	By

Form 2

FAMILY GROUP RECORD

	Wife			Husband	
		Name			
		Born			
		Married			
		Died			
		Burial			
		Father			
		Mother			
	husband	Other (if any)	wife		

Notes

Date married & spouse

#	Sex	Children in order of birth	Born Day Month Year	Where born	Died Day Month Year	Where died

Source   By

Form 2

FAMILY GROUP RECORD

	Wife			Husband	
			Name		
			Born		
			Married		
			Died		
			Burial		
			Father		
			Mother		
	husband	Other (if any)	wife		

Notes

Date married & spouse

#	Sex	Children in order of birth	Born Day Month Year	Where born	Died Day Month Year	Where died

Source	By

Form 2

FAMILY GROUP RECORD

	Wife			Husband	
		Name			
		Born			
		Married			
		Died			
		Burial			
		Father			
		Mother			
	husband	Other (if any)	wife		

Notes

Date married & spouse

#	Sex	Children in order of birth	Born Day Month Year	Where born	Died Day Month Year	Where died

Source   By

Form 2

FAMILY GROUP RECORD

	Wife			Husband
		Name		
		Born		
		Married		
		Died		
		Burial		
		Father		
		Mother		
	husband	Other (if any)	wife	

Notes

Date married & spouse

#	Sex	Children in order of birth	Born Day Month Year	Where born	Died Day Month Year	Where died

Source _____ By _____

Form 2

FAMILY GROUP RECORD

	Wife			Husband	
			Name		
			Born		
			Married		
			Died		
			Burial		
			Father		
			Mother		
		husband	Other (if any)	wife	

Notes

Date married & spouse

#	Sex	Children in order of birth	Born Day Month Year	Where born	Died Day Month Year	Where died

Source	By

Form 2

FAMILY GROUP RECORD

	Wife		Husband
		Name	
		Born	
		Married	
		Died	
		Burial	
		Father	
		Mother	
	husband	Other (if any)	wife

Notes

Date married & spouse

#	Sex	Children in order of birth	Born Day Month Year	Where born	Died Day Month Year	Where died

Source   By

HISTORY SHEET

Surname:

Given name:

Date of record:

Source:

HISTORY SHEET

Surname:

Given name:

Date of record:

Source:

HISTORY SHEET

Surname:

Given name:

Date of record:

Source:

HISTORY SHEET

Surname:

Given name:

Date of record:

Source:

HISTORY SHEET

Surname:

Given name:

Date of record:

Source:

HISTORY SHEET

Surname:

Given name:

Date of record:

Source:

HISTORY SHEET

Surname:

Given name:

Date of record:

Source:

HISTORY SHEET

Surname:

Given name:

Date of record:

Source:

HISTORY SHEET

Surname:

Given name:

Date of record:

Source:

HISTORY SHEET

Surname:

Given name:

Date of record:

Source:

HISTORY SHEET

Surname:

Given name:

Date of record:

Source:

HISTORY SHEET

Surname:

Given name:

Date of record:

Source:

HISTORY SHEET

Surname:

Given name:

Date of record:

Source:

HISTORY SHEET

Surname:

Given name:

Date of record:

Source:

HISTORY SHEET

Surname:

Given name:

Date of record:

Source:

HISTORY SHEET

Surname:

Given name:

Date of record:

Source:

HISTORY SHEET

Surname:

Given name:

Date of record:

Source:

HISTORY SHEET

Surname:

Given name:

Date of record:

Source:

HISTORY SHEET

Surname:

Given name:

Date of record:

Source:

HISTORY SHEET

Surname:

Given name:

Date of record:

Source:

HISTORY SHEET

Surname:

Given name:

Date of record:

Source:

HISTORY SHEET

Surname:

Given name:

Date of record:

Source:

HISTORY SHEET

Surname:

Given name:

Date of record:

Source:

HISTORY SHEET

Surname:

Given name:

Date of record:

Source:

RESEARCH CHECK LIST

m.:

m(2):

Name:
Relationship:
Inclusive dates:
Parents:

Location of sources:	Type of source:	Date of source:	Location of notes:
Home	Family Bible		
	Family letters		
	Interviews		
	Photographs		
County records	Vital records		
	Marriage records		
	Wills, estates, etc.		
	Deeds, etc.		
	Mortgages		
	Other recorders' records		
	Naturalization records		
Town records and libraries	City or county directories		
	Cemetery records/grave. insc.		
	Ms. or pub. histories		
	Newspaper files		
	Tax lists		
	Voter records		
	Public school records		
Church depositories	Archives		
	Local parish records		
	Local church histories		
State records	Vital records		
	Land grants		
	State census		
	Militia records		
	Tax lists		
	Archives		
	Acts, journals		
National records	Censuses		
	Mortality schedules		
	Military records		
	Pension records		
	Passenger lists		
	Immigration records		
	Land records		
	Special records		
Libraries	Indexes, special		
	Printed & ms. genealogies		
	Printed histories		
	Occupational histories		
	Biographical compendia		
	Manuscript histories		
	Obituary collections/indexes		
	Cemetery records/grave. insc.		
	Abstract volumes		
Correspondence			

RESEARCH CHECK LIST

m.:

m(2):

Name:

Relationship:

Inclusive dates:

Parents:

Location of sources:	Type of source:	Date of source:	Location of notes:
Home	Family Bible		
	Family letters		
	Interviews		
	Photographs		
County records	Vital records		
	Marriage records		
	Wills, estates, etc.		
	Deeds, etc.		
	Mortgages		
	Other recorders' records		
	Naturalization records		
Town records and libraries	City or county directories		
	Cemetery records/grave. insc.		
	Ms. or pub. histories		
	Newspaper files		
	Tax lists		
	Voter records		
	Public school records		
Church depositories	Archives		
	Local parish records		
	Local church histories		
State records	Vital records		
	Land grants		
	State census		
	Militia records		
	Tax lists		
	Archives		
	Acts, journals		
National records	Censuses		
	Mortality schedules		
	Military records		
	Pension records		
	Passenger lists		
	Immigration records		
	Land records		
	Special records		
Libraries	Indexes, special		
	Printed & ms. genealogies		
	Printed histories		
	Occupational histories		
	Biographical compendia		
	Manuscript histories		
	Obituary collections/indexes		
	Cemetery records/grave. insc.		
	Abstract volumes		
Correspondence			

RESEARCH CHECK LIST

m.:

m(2):

Name:

Relationship:

Inclusive dates:

Parents:

Location of sources:	Type of source:	Date of source:	Location of notes:
Home	Family Bible		
	Family letters		
	Interviews		
	Photographs		
County records	Vital records		
	Marriage records		
	Wills, estates, etc.		
	Deeds, etc.		
	Mortgages		
	Other recorders' records		
	Naturalization records		
Town records and libraries	City or county directories		
	Cemetery records/grave. insc.		
	Ms. or pub. histories		
	Newspaper files		
	Tax lists		
	Voter records		
	Public school records		
Church depositories	Archives		
	Local parish records		
	Local church histories		
State records	Vital records		
	Land grants		
	State census		
	Militia records		
	Tax lists		
	Archives		
	Acts, journals		
National records	Censuses		
	Mortality schedules		
	Military records		
	Pension records		
	Passenger lists		
	Immigration records		
	Land records		
	Special records		
Libraries	Indexes, special		
	Printed & ms. genealogies		
	Printed histories		
	Occupational histories		
	Biographical compendia		
	Manuscript histories		
	Obituary collections/indexes		
	Cemetery records/grave. insc.		
	Abstract volumes		
Correspondence			

RESEARCH CHECK LIST

m.:

m(2):

Name:
Relationship:
Inclusive dates:
Parents:

Location of sources:	Type of source:	Date of source:	Location of notes:
Home	Family Bible		
	Family letters		
	Interviews		
	Photographs		
County records	Vital records		
	Marriage records		
	Wills, estates, etc.		
	Deeds, etc.		
	Mortgages		
	Other recorders' records		
	Naturalization records		
Town records and libraries	City or county directories		
	Cemetery records/grave. insc.		
	Ms. or pub. histories		
	Newspaper files		
	Tax lists		
	Voter records		
	Public school records		
Church depositories	Archives		
	Local parish records		
	Local church histories		
State records	Vital records		
	Land grants		
	State census		
	Militia records		
	Tax lists		
	Archives		
	Acts, journals		
National records	Censuses		
	Mortality schedules		
	Military records		
	Pension records		
	Passenger lists		
	Immigration records		
	Land records		
	Special records		
Libraries	Indexes, special		
	Printed & ms. genealogies		
	Printed histories		
	Occupational histories		
	Biographical compendia		
	Manuscript histories		
	Obituary collections/indexes		
	Cemetery records/grave. insc.		
	Abstract volumes		
Correspondence			

Form 4

RESEARCH CHECK LIST

m.:

m(2):

Name:
Relationship:
Inclusive dates:
Parents:

Location of sources:	*Type of source:*	*Date of source:*	*Location of notes:*
Home	Family Bible		
	Family letters		
	Interviews		
	Photographs		
County records	Vital records		
	Marriage records		
	Wills, estates, etc.		
	Deeds, etc.		
	Mortgages		
	Other recorders' records		
	Naturalization records		
Town records and libraries	City or county directories		
	Cemetery records/grave. insc.		
	Ms. or pub. histories		
	Newspaper files		
	Tax lists		
	Voter records		
	Public school records		
Church depositories	Archives		
	Local parish records		
	Local church histories		
State records	Vital records		
	Land grants		
	State census		
	Militia records		
	Tax lists		
	Archives		
	Acts, journals		
National records	Censuses		
	Mortality schedules		
	Military records		
	Pension records		
	Passenger lists		
	Immigration records		
	Land records		
	Special records		
Libraries	Indexes, special		
	Printed & ms. genealogies		
	Printed histories		
	Occupational histories		
	Biographical compendia		
	Manuscript histories		
	Obituary collections/indexes		
	Cemetery records/grave. insc.		
	Abstract volumes		
Correspondence			

RESEARCH CHECK LIST

m.:

m(2):

Name:
Relationship:
Inclusive dates:
Parents:

Location of sources:	*Type of source:*	*Date of source:*	*Location of notes:*
Home	Family Bible		
	Family letters		
	Interviews		
	Photographs		
County records	Vital records		
	Marriage records		
	Wills, estates, etc.		
	Deeds, etc.		
	Mortgages		
	Other recorders' records		
	Naturalization records		
Town records and libraries	City or county directories		
	Cemetery records/grave. insc.		
	Ms. or pub. histories		
	Newspaper files		
	Tax lists		
	Voter records		
	Public school records		
Church depositories	Archives		
	Local parish records		
	Local church histories		
State records	Vital records		
	Land grants		
	State census		
	Militia records		
	Tax lists		
	Archives		
	Acts, journals		
National records	Censuses		
	Mortality schedules		
	Military records		
	Pension records		
	Passenger lists		
	Immigration records		
	Land records		
	Special records		
Libraries	Indexes, special		
	Printed & ms. genealogies		
	Printed histories		
	Occupational histories		
	Biographical compendia		
	Manuscript histories		
	Obituary collections/indexes		
	Cemetery records/grave. insc.		
	Abstract volumes		
Correspondence			

RESEARCH CHECK LIST

m.:

m(2):

Name:
Relationship:
Inclusive dates:
Parents:

Location of sources:	*Type of source:*	*Date of source:*	*Location of notes:*
Home	Family Bible		
	Family letters		
	Interviews		
	Photographs		
County records	Vital records		
	Marriage records		
	Wills, estates, etc.		
	Deeds, etc.		
	Mortgages		
	Other recorders' records		
	Naturalization records		
Town records and libraries	City or county directories		
	Cemetery records/grave. insc.		
	Ms. or pub. histories		
	Newspaper files		
	Tax lists		
	Voter records		
	Public school records		
Church depositories	Archives		
	Local parish records		
	Local church histories		
State records	Vital records		
	Land grants		
	State census		
	Militia records		
	Tax lists		
	Archives		
	Acts, journals		
National records	Censuses		
	Mortality schedules		
	Military records		
	Pension records		
	Passenger lists		
	Immigration records		
	Land records		
	Special records		
Libraries	Indexes, special		
	Printed & ms. genealogies		
	Printed histories		
	Occupational histories		
	Biographical compendia		
	Manuscript histories		
	Obituary collections/indexes		
	Cemetery records/grave. insc.		
	Abstract volumes		
Correspondence			

Form 4

RESEARCH CHECK LIST

m.:

m(2):

Name:
Relationship:
Inclusive dates:
Parents:

Location of sources:	Type of source:	Date of source:	Location of notes:
Home	Family Bible		
	Family letters		
	Interviews		
	Photographs		
County records	Vital records		
	Marriage records		
	Wills, estates, etc.		
	Deeds, etc.		
	Mortgages		
	Other recorders' records		
	Naturalization records		
Town records and libraries	City or county directories		
	Cemetery records/grave. insc.		
	Ms. or pub. histories		
	Newspaper files		
	Tax lists		
	Voter records		
	Public school records		
Church depositories	Archives		
	Local parish records		
	Local church histories		
State records	Vital records		
	Land grants		
	State census		
	Militia records		
	Tax lists		
	Archives		
	Acts, journals		
National records	Censuses		
	Mortality schedules		
	Military records		
	Pension records		
	Passenger lists		
	Immigration records		
	Land records		
	Special records		
Libraries	Indexes, special		
	Printed & ms. genealogies		
	Printed histories		
	Occupational histories		
	Biographical compendia		
	Manuscript histories		
	Obituary collections/indexes		
	Cemetery records/grave. insc.		
	Abstract volumes		
Correspondence			

RESEARCH CHECK LIST

m.:

m(2):

Name:
Relationship:
Inclusive dates:
Parents:

Location of sources:	*Type of source:*	*Date of source:*	*Location of notes:*
Home	Family Bible		
	Family letters		
	Interviews		
	Photographs		
County records	Vital records		
	Marriage records		
	Wills, estates, etc.		
	Deeds, etc.		
	Mortgages		
	Other recorders' records		
	Naturalization records		
Town records and libraries	City or county directories		
	Cemetery records/grave. insc.		
	Ms. or pub. histories		
	Newspaper files		
	Tax lists		
	Voter records		
	Public school records		
Church depositories	Archives		
	Local parish records		
	Local church histories		
State records	Vital records		
	Land grants		
	State census		
	Militia records		
	Tax lists		
	Archives		
	Acts, journals		
National records	Censuses		
	Mortality schedules		
	Military records		
	Pension records		
	Passenger lists		
	Immigration records		
	Land records		
	Special records		
Libraries	Indexes, special		
	Printed & ms. genealogies		
	Printed histories		
	Occupational histories		
	Biographical compendia		
	Manuscript histories		
	Obituary collections/indexes		
	Cemetery records/grave. insc.		
	Abstract volumes		
Correspondence			

Form 4

RESEARCH CHECK LIST

m.:

m(2):

Name:
Relationship:
Inclusive dates:
Parents:

Location of sources:	*Type of source:*	*Date of source:*	*Location of notes:*
Home	Family Bible		
	Family letters		
	Interviews		
	Photographs		
County records	Vital records		
	Marriage records		
	Wills, estates, etc.		
	Deeds, etc.		
	Mortgages		
	Other recorders' records		
	Naturalization records		
Town records and libraries	City or county directories		
	Cemetery records/grave. insc.		
	Ms. or pub. histories		
	Newspaper files		
	Tax lists		
	Voter records		
	Public school records		
Church depositories	Archives		
	Local parish records		
	Local church histories		
State records	Vital records		
	Land grants		
	State census		
	Militia records		
	Tax lists		
	Archives		
	Acts, journals		
National records	Censuses		
	Mortality schedules		
	Military records		
	Pension records		
	Passenger lists		
	Immigration records		
	Land records		
	Special records		
Libraries	Indexes, special		
	Printed & ms. genealogies		
	Printed histories		
	Occupational histories		
	Biographical compendia		
	Manuscript histories		
	Obituary collections/indexes		
	Cemetery records/grave. insc.		
	Abstract volumes		
Correspondence			

RESEARCH CHECK LIST

m.:

m(2):

Name:
Relationship:
Inclusive dates:
Parents:

Location of sources:	*Type of source:*	*Date of source:*	*Location of notes:*
Home	Family Bible		
	Family letters		
	Interviews		
	Photographs		
County records	Vital records		
	Marriage records		
	Wills, estates, etc.		
	Deeds, etc.		
	Mortgages		
	Other recorders' records		
	Naturalization records		
Town records and libraries	City or county directories		
	Cemetery records/grave. insc.		
	Ms. or pub. histories		
	Newspaper files		
	Tax lists		
	Voter records		
	Public school records		
Church depositories	Archives		
	Local parish records		
	Local church histories		
State records	Vital records		
	Land grants		
	State census		
	Militia records		
	Tax lists		
	Archives		
	Acts, journals		
National records	Censuses		
	Mortality schedules		
	Military records		
	Pension records		
	Passenger lists		
	Immigration records		
	Land records		
	Special records		
Libraries	Indexes, special		
	Printed & ms. genealogies		
	Printed histories		
	Occupational histories		
	Biographical compendia		
	Manuscript histories		
	Obituary collections/indexes		
	Cemetery records/grave. insc.		
	Abstract volumes		
Correspondence			

RESEARCH CHECK LIST

m.:   Name:
                                       Relationship:
m(2):   Inclusive dates:
                                       Parents:

Location of sources:	*Type of source:*	*Date of source:*	*Location of notes:*
Home	Family Bible		
	Family letters		
	Interviews		
	Photographs		
County records	Vital records		
	Marriage records		
	Wills, estates, etc.		
	Deeds, etc.		
	Mortgages		
	Other recorders' records		
	Naturalization records		
Town records and libraries	City or county directories		
	Cemetery records/grave. insc.		
	Ms. or pub. histories		
	Newspaper files		
	Tax lists		
	Voter records		
	Public school records		
Church depositories	Archives		
	Local parish records		
	Local church histories		
State records	Vital records		
	Land grants		
	State census		
	Militia records		
	Tax lists		
	Archives		
	Acts, journals		
National records	Censuses		
	Mortality schedules		
	Military records		
	Pension records		
	Passenger lists		
	Immigration records		
	Land records		
	Special records		
Libraries	Indexes, special		
	Printed & ms. genealogies		
	Printed histories		
	Occupational histories		
	Biographical compendia		
	Manuscript histories		
	Obituary collections/indexes		
	Cemetery records/grave. insc.		
	Abstract volumes		
Correspondence			

RESEARCH CHECK LIST

m.:

m(2):

Name:
Relationship:
Inclusive dates:
Parents:

Location of sources:	*Type of source:*	*Date of source:*	*Location of notes:*
Home	Family Bible		
	Family letters		
	Interviews		
	Photographs		
County records	Vital records		
	Marriage records		
	Wills, estates, etc.		
	Deeds, etc.		
	Mortgages		
	Other recorders' records		
	Naturalization records		
Town records and libraries	City or county directories		
	Cemetery records/grave. insc.		
	Ms. or pub. histories		
	Newspaper files		
	Tax lists		
	Voter records		
	Public school records		
Church depositories	Archives		
	Local parish records		
	Local church histories		
State records	Vital records		
	Land grants		
	State census		
	Militia records		
	Tax lists		
	Archives		
	Acts, journals		
National records	Censuses		
	Mortality schedules		
	Military records		
	Pension records		
	Passenger lists		
	Immigration records		
	Land records		
	Special records		
Libraries	Indexes, special		
	Printed & ms. genealogies		
	Printed histories		
	Occupational histories		
	Biographical compendia		
	Manuscript histories		
	Obituary collections/indexes		
	Cemetery records/grave. insc.		
	Abstract volumes		
Correspondence			

RESEARCH CHECK LIST

m.:

m(2):

Name:
Relationship:
Inclusive dates:
Parents:

Location of sources:	*Type of source:*	*Date of source:*	*Location of notes:*
Home	Family Bible		
	Family letters		
	Interviews		
	Photographs		
County records	Vital records		
	Marriage records		
	Wills, estates, etc.		
	Deeds, etc.		
	Mortgages		
	Other recorders' records		
	Naturalization records		
Town records and libraries	City or county directories		
	Cemetery records/grave. insc.		
	Ms. or pub. histories		
	Newspaper files		
	Tax lists		
	Voter records		
	Public school records		
Church depositories	Archives		
	Local parish records		
	Local church histories		
State records	Vital records		
	Land grants		
	State census		
	Militia records		
	Tax lists		
	Archives		
	Acts, journals		
National records	Censuses		
	Mortality schedules		
	Military records		
	Pension records		
	Passenger lists		
	Immigration records		
	Land records		
	Special records		
Libraries	Indexes, special		
	Printed & ms. genealogies		
	Printed histories		
	Occupational histories		
	Biographical compendia		
	Manuscript histories		
	Obituary collections/indexes		
	Cemetery records/grave. insc.		
	Abstract volumes		
Correspondence			

RESEARCH CHECK LIST

m.:

m(2):

Name:
Relationship:
Inclusive dates:
Parents:

Location of sources:	Type of source:	Date of source:	Location of notes:
Home	Family Bible		
	Family letters		
	Interviews		
	Photographs		
County records	Vital records		
	Marriage records		
	Wills, estates, etc.		
	Deeds, etc.		
	Mortgages		
	Other recorders' records		
	Naturalization records		
Town records and libraries	City or county directories		
	Cemetery records/grave. insc.		
	Ms. or pub. histories		
	Newspaper files		
	Tax lists		
	Voter records		
	Public school records		
Church depositories	Archives		
	Local parish records		
	Local church histories		
State records	Vital records		
	Land grants		
	State census		
	Militia records		
	Tax lists		
	Archives		
	Acts, journals		
National records	Censuses		
	Mortality schedules		
	Military records		
	Pension records		
	Passenger lists		
	Immigration records		
	Land records		
	Special records		
Libraries	Indexes, special		
	Printed & ms. genealogies		
	Printed histories		
	Occupational histories		
	Biographical compendia		
	Manuscript histories		
	Obituary collections/indexes		
	Cemetery records/grave. insc.		
	Abstract volumes		
Correspondence			

RESEARCH CHECK LIST

m.:

m(2):

Name:
Relationship:
Inclusive dates:
Parents:

Location of sources:	*Type of source:*	*Date of source:*	*Location of notes:*
Home	Family Bible		
	Family letters		
	Interviews		
	Photographs		
County records	Vital records		
	Marriage records		
	Wills, estates, etc.		
	Deeds, etc.		
	Mortgages		
	Other recorders' records		
	Naturalization records		
Town records and libraries	City or county directories		
	Cemetery records/grave. insc.		
	Ms. or pub. histories		
	Newspaper files		
	Tax lists		
	Voter records		
	Public school records		
Church depositories	Archives		
	Local parish records		
	Local church histories		
State records	Vital records		
	Land grants		
	State census		
	Militia records		
	Tax lists		
	Archives		
	Acts, journals		
National records	Censuses		
	Mortality schedules		
	Military records		
	Pension records		
	Passenger lists		
	Immigration records		
	Land records		
	Special records		
Libraries	Indexes, special		
	Printed & ms. genealogies		
	Printed histories		
	Occupational histories		
	Biographical compendia		
	Manuscript histories		
	Obituary collections/indexes		
	Cemetery records/grave. insc.		
	Abstract volumes		
Correspondence			

SEARCH CONTROL RECORD

Surnames:

Sources to consult:

Form 5

SEARCH CONTROL RECORD

Surnames:

Sources to consult:

Form 5

SEARCH CONTROL RECORD

Surnames:

Sources to consult:

SEARCH CONTROL RECORD

Surnames:

Sources to consult:

SEARCH CONTROL RECORD

Surnames:

Sources to consult:

SEARCH CONTROL RECORD

Surnames:

Sources to consult:

SEARCH CONTROL RECORD

Surnames:

Sources to consult:

Form 5

SEARCH CONTROL RECORD

Surnames:

Sources to consult:

SEARCH CONTROL RECORD

Surnames:

Sources to consult:

Form 5

SEARCH CONTROL RECORD

Surnames:

Sources to consult:

Form 5

EXTRACT FROM 1800 OR 1810 CENSUS

State _____ County or Parish _____ Township, Ward or Beat _____ Post Office _____

Index compiled by _____ Extract by _____ Date of Enumeration _____ Publication No. _____ Reel No. _____

Page	Names of heads of families	Free white persons, including heads of families												All other free persons except Indians	Slaves
		Males						Females							
		To 10	10–16	16–26	26–45	45 up	To 10	10–16	16–26	26–45	45 up				

Form 6

EXTRACT FROM 1800 OR 1810 CENSUS

State _____ County or Parish _____ Post Office _____

Index compiled by _____ Extract by _____ Township, Ward or Beat _____ Publication No. _____ Reel No. _____

Date of Enumeration _____

Page	Names of heads of families	Free white persons, including heads of families										All other free persons except Indians	Slaves
		Males					Females						
		To 10	10–16	16–26	26–45	45 up	To 10	10–16	16–26	26–45	45 up		

Form 6

EXTRACT FROM 1800 OR 1810 CENSUS

State_____ County or Parish_____ Township, Ward or Beat_____ Post Office_____

Index compiled by_____ Extract by_____ Date of Enumeration_____ Publication No._____ Reel No._____

Page	Names of heads of families	Free white persons, including heads of families										All other free persons except Indians	Slaves
		Males					Females						
		To 10	10-16	16-26	26-45	45 up	To 10	10-16	16-26	26-45	45 up		

Form 6

EXTRACT FROM 1800 OR 1810 CENSUS

State _____ County or Parish _____ Extract by _____ Township, Ward or Beat _____ Date of Enumeration _____ Post Office _____ Publication No. _____ Reel No. _____

Index compiled by _____

Page	Names of heads of families	Free white persons, including heads of families										All other free persons except Indians	Slaves
		Males					Females						
		To 10	10–16	16–26	26–45	45 up	To 10	10–16	16–26	26–45	45 up		

Form 6

EXTRACT FROM 1820 CENSUS

State_____ County or Parish_____ Township, Ward or Beat_____ Post Office_____

Index compiled by_____ Extract by_____ Date of Enumeration_____ Publication No._____ Reel No._____

Page	Head of family	Residence	Males						Females					Foreigners not naturalized	No. persons engaged in:			Slaves								Free colored persons								All other persons
			To 10	10-16	16-18	16-26	26-45	45 up	To 10	10-16	16-26	26-45	45 up		Agriculture	Commerce	Manufacture	Males				Females				Males				Females				
																		To 14	14-26	26-45	45 up	To 14	14-26	26-45	45 up	To 14	14-26	26-45	45 up	To 14	14-26	26-45	45 up	

Form 7

EXTRACT FROM 1820 CENSUS

State _____ County or Parish _____ Township, Ward or Beat _____ Post Office _____

Index compiled by _____ Extract by _____ Date of Enumeration _____ Publication No. _____ Reel No. _____

Page	Head of family	Residence	Males						Females					Foreigners not naturalized	No. persons engaged in:			Slaves								Free colored persons								All other persons
			To 10	10-16	16-18	16-26	26-45	45 up	To 10	10-16	16-26	26-45	45 up		Agriculture	Commerce	Manufacture	Males				Females				Males				Females				
																		To 14	14-26	26-45	45 up	To 14	14-26	26-45	45 up	To 14	14-26	26-45	45 up	To 14	14-26	26-45	45 up	

EXTRACT FROM 1820 CENSUS

State_____ County or Parish_____ Township, Ward or Beat_____ Post Office_____

Index compiled by_____ Extract by_____ Date of Enumeration_____ Publication No._____ Reel No._____

Page	Head of family	Residence	Males						Females						Foreigners not naturalized	No. persons engaged in: Agriculture	No. persons engaged in: Commerce	No. persons engaged in: Manufacture	Slaves Males				Slaves Females				Free colored persons Males				Free colored persons Females				All other persons
			To 10	10-16	16-18	16-26	26-45	45 up	To 10	10-16	16-26	26-45	45 up						To 14	14-26	26-45	45 up	To 14	14-26	26-45	45 up	To 14	14-26	26-45	45 up	To 14	14-26	26-45	45 up	

Form 7

EXTRACT FROM 1820 CENSUS

State_____ County or Parish_____ Township, Ward or Beat_____ Post Office_____

Index compiled by_____ Extract by_____ Date of Enumeration_____ Publication No._____ Reel No._____

Page	Head of family	Residence	Males						Females					Foreigners not naturalized	No. persons engaged in:			Slaves									Free colored persons								All other persons
			To 10	10–16	16–18	16–26	26–45	45 up	To 10	10–16	16–26	26–45	45 up		Agriculture	Commerce	Manufacture	\<Males\> To 14	14–26	26–45	45 up	\<Females\> To 14	14–26	26–45	45 up		\<Males\> To 14	14–26	26–45	45 up	\<Females\> To 14	14–26	26–45	45 up	

Form 7

EXTRACT FROM 1830 OR 1840 CENSUS

State _____ County or Parish _____ Township, Ward or Beat _____ Post Office _____

Index compiled by _____ Extract by _____ Date of Enumeration _____ Publication No. _____ Reel No. _____

Page	Names of heads of families	Free white persons, including heads of families																										Employment — Pensioners	Impairment — Schools
		Males												Females														
		To 5	5-10	10-15	15-20	20-30	30-40	40-50	50-60	60-70	70-80	80-90	90-100	To 5	5-10	10-15	15-20	20-30	30-40	40-50	50-60	60-70	70-80	80-90	90-100		

Form 8

EXTRACT FROM 1830 OR 1840 CENSUS

State _____ County or Parish _____ Township, Ward or Beat _____ Post Office _____

Index compiled by _____ Extract by _____ Date of Enumeration _____ Publication No. _____ Reel No. _____

Page	Names of heads of families	Free white persons, including heads of families																										Employment / Pensioners	Impairment / Schools
		Males												Females														
		To 5	5-10	10-15	15-20	20-30	30-40	40-50	50-60	60-70	70-80	80-90	90-100	To 5	5-10	10-15	15-20	20-30	30-40	40-50	50-60	60-70	70-80	80-90	90-100		

Form 8

EXTRACT FROM 1830 OR 1840 CENSUS

State_____ County or Parish_____ Township, Ward or Beat_____ Post Office_____ Reel No._____

Index compiled by_____ Extract by_____ Date of Enumeration_____ Publication No._____

Page	Names of heads of families	Free white persons, including heads of families																										Employment — Pensioners	Impairment — Schools
		Males												Females														
		To 5	5-10	10-15	15-20	20-30	30-40	40-50	50-60	60-70	70-80	80-90	90-100	To 5	5-10	10-15	15-20	20-30	30-40	40-50	50-60	60-70	70-80	80-90	90-100		

EXTRACT FROM 1830 OR 1840 CENSUS

State_____ County or Parish_____ Township, Ward or Beat_____ Post Office_____

Index compiled by_____ Extract by_____ Date of Enumeration_____ Publication No._____ Reel No._____

Page	Names of heads of families	Free white persons, including heads of families																											Employment — Pensioners	Impairment — Schools
		Males													Females														
		To 5	5–10	10–15	15–20	20–30	30–40	40–50	50–60	60–70	70–80	80–90	90–100		To 5	5–10	10–15	15–20	20–30	30–40	40–50	50–60	60–70	70–80	80–90	90–100		

Form 8

EXTRACT FROM 1850 CENSUS

State _____ County or Parish _____ Township, Ward or Beat _____ Post Office _____

Index compiled by _____ Extract by _____ Date of Enumeration _____ Publication No. _____ Reel No. _____

Page	Dwelling No.	Family No.	Names	Age	Sex	Color	Occupation, etc.	Value of real estate	Birthplace	Married within year	School within year	Cannot read or write	Remarks

Form 9

EXTRACT FROM 1850 CENSUS

State _____ County or Parish _____ Township, Ward or Beat _____ Post Office _____

Index compiled by _____ Extract by _____ Date of Enumeration _____ Publication No. _____ Reel No. _____

Page	Dwelling No.	Family No.	Names	Age	Sex	Color	Occupation, etc.	Value of real estate	Birthplace	Married within year	School within year	Cannot read or write	Remarks

Form 9

EXTRACT FROM 1850 CENSUS

State_____ County or Parish_____ Township, Ward or Beat_____ Post Office_____

Index compiled by_____ Extract by_____ Date of Enumeration_____ Publication No._____ Reel No._____

Page	Dwelling No.	Family No.	Names	Age	Sex	Color	Occupation, etc.	Value of real estate	Birthplace	Married within year	School within year	Cannot read or write	Remarks

Form 9

EXTRACT FROM 1850 CENSUS

State_____ County or Parish_____ Township, Ward or Beat_____ Post Office_____

Index compiled by_____ Extract by_____ Date of Enumeration_____ Publication No._____ Reel No._____

Page	Dwelling No.	Family No.	Names	Age	Sex	Color	Occupation, etc.	Value of real estate	Birthplace	Married within year	School within year	Cannot read or write	Remarks

EXTRACT FROM 1860 CENSUS

State _____ County or Parish _____ Township, Ward or Beat _____ Post Office _____ Reel No. _____

Index compiled by _____ Extract by _____ Date of Enumeration _____ Publication No. _____

Page	Dwelling No.	Family No.	Names	Age	Sex	Color	Occupation, etc.	Value of real estate	Value of personal property	Birthplace	Married in year	School in year	Cannot read or write	Remarks

Form 10

EXTRACT FROM 1860 CENSUS

State _____ County or Parish _____ Township, Ward or Beat _____ Post Office _____

Index compiled by _____ Extract by _____ Date of Enumeration _____ Publication No. _____ Reel No. _____

Page	Dwelling No.	Family No.	Names	Age	Sex	Color	Occupation, etc.	Value of real estate	Value of personal property	Birthplace	Married in year	School in year	Cannot read or write	Remarks

Form 10

EXTRACT FROM 1860 CENSUS

State _____ County or Parish _____ Township, Ward or Beat _____ Post Office _____

Index compiled by _____ Extract by _____ Date of Enumeration _____ Publication No. _____ Reel No. _____

Page	Dwelling No.	Family No.	Names	Age	Sex	Color	Occupation, etc.	Value of real estate	Value of personal property	Birthplace	Married in year	School in year	Cannot read or write	Remarks

Form 10

EXTRACT FROM 1860 CENSUS

State _____ County or Parish _____ Township, Ward or Beat _____ Post Office _____

Index compiled by _____ Extract by _____ Date of Enumeration _____ Publication No. _____ Reel No. _____

Page	Dwelling No.	Family No.	Names	Age	Sex	Color	Occupation, etc.	Value of real estate	Value of personal property	Birthplace	Married in year	School in year	Cannot read or write	Remarks

Form 10

EXTRACT FROM 1870 CENSUS

State_____ County or Parish_____ Township, Ward or Beat_____ Post Office_____

Index compiled by_____ Extract by_____ Date of Enumeration_____ Publication No._____ Reel No._____

Page	Dwelling No.	Family No.	Names	Age	Sex	Color	Occupation, etc.	Value of real estate	Value of personal property	Birthplace	Father foreign born	Mother foreign born	Month born in year	Month married in year	School in year	Cannot read	Cannot write	Impairment	Males eligible to vote	Males ineligible to vote

Form 11

EXTRACT FROM 1870 CENSUS

State _____ County or Parish _____ Township, Ward or Beat _____ Post Office _____

Index compiled by _____ Extract by _____ Date of Enumeration _____ Publication No. _____ Reel No. _____

Page	Dwelling No.	Family No.	Names	Age	Sex	Color	Occupation, etc.	Value of real estate	Value of personal property	Birthplace	Father foreign born	Mother foreign born	Month born in year	Month married in year	School in year	Cannot read	Cannot write	Impairment	Males eligible to vote	Males ineligible to vote

Form 11

EXTRACT FROM 1870 CENSUS

State _____ County or Parish _____ Township, Ward or Beat _____ Post Office _____

Index compiled by _____ Extract by _____ Date of Enumeration _____ Publication No. _____ Reel No. _____

Page	Dwelling No.	Family No.	Names	Age	Sex	Color	Occupation, etc.	Value of real estate	Value of personal property	Birthplace	Father foreign born	Mother foreign born	Month born in year	Month married in year	School in year	Cannot read	Cannot write	Impairment	Males eligible to vote	Males ineligible to vote

Form 11

EXTRACT FROM 1870 CENSUS

State _____ County or Parish _____ Township, Ward or Beat _____ Post Office _____

Index compiled by _____ Extract by _____ Date of Enumeration _____ Publication No. _____ Reel No. _____

Page	Dwelling No.	Family No.	Names	Age	Sex	Color	Occupation, etc.	Value of real estate	Value of personal property	Birthplace	Father foreign born	Mother foreign born	Month born in year	Month married in year	School in year	Cannot read	Cannot write	Impairment	Males eligible to vote	Males ineligible to vote

Form 11

EXTRACT FROM 1880 CENSUS

State _____ County or Parish _____ Township, Ward or Beat _____ Sup. Dist. No. _____ Enum. Dist. No. _____

Index compiled by _____ Extract by _____ Date of Enumeration _____ Publication No. _____ Reel No. _____

Page	Dwelling No.	Family No.	Names	Color	Sex	Age prior to June 1st	Month of birth if born in census year	Relationship to head of house	Single	Married	Widowed/Divorced	Married in census year	Occupation	Miscellaneous	Cannot read	Cannot write	Place of birth	Place of birth of father	Place of birth of mother

Form 12

EXTRACT FROM 1880 CENSUS

State_____ County or Parish_____ Township, Ward or Beat_____ Sup. Dist. No._____ Enum. Dist. No._____

Index compiled by_____ Extract by_____ Date of Enumeration_____ Publication No._____ Reel No._____

Page	Dwelling No.	Family No.	Names	Color	Sex	Age prior to June 1st	Month of birth if born in census year	Relationship to head of house	Single	Married	Widowed/Divorced	Married in census year	Occupation	Miscellaneous	Cannot read	Cannot write	Place of birth	Place of birth of father	Place of birth of mother

Form 12

EXTRACT FROM 1900 CENSUS

State _____ County or Parish _____ Township, Ward or Beat _____ Street _____

Index compiled by _____ Extract by _____ Date of Enumeration _____ Publication No. _____ Reel No. _____

Enumeration district	House No.	Sheet	Line	Names	Relationship to head of house	Color	Sex	Month and year of birth	Age	Marital status	Years married	Mother of how many children	No. of these children living	Person's birthplace	Father's birthplace	Mother's birthplace	Year of immigration	No. of years in U.S.	Naturalized	Occupation	Remarks

Form 13

EXTRACT FROM 1900 CENSUS

State _____ County or Parish _____ Township, Ward or Beat _____ Street _____

Index compiled by _____ Extract by _____ Date of Enumeration _____ Publication No. _____ Reel No. _____

Enumeration district	House No.	Sheet	Line	Names	Relationship to head of house	Color	Sex	Month and year of birth	Age	Marital status	Years married	Mother of how many children	No. of these children living	Person's birthplace	Father's birthplace	Mother's birthplace	Year of immigration	No. of years in U.S.	Naturalized	Occupation	Remarks

Form 13

EXTRACT FROM 1900 CENSUS

State _____ County or Parish _____ Township, Ward or Beat _____ Street _____

Index compiled by _____ Extract by _____ Date of Enumeration _____ Publication No. _____ Reel No. _____

Enumeration district	House No.	Sheet	Line	Names	Relationship to head of house	Color	Sex	Month and year of birth	Age	Marital status	Years married	Mother of how many children	No. of these children living	Person's birthplace	Father's birthplace	Mother's birthplace	Year of immigration	No. of years in U.S.	Naturalized	Occupation	Remarks

Form 13

EXTRACT FROM 1910 CENSUS

Extract by _____

State _____ County or Parish _____ Township, Ward or Beat _____ Incorporated Place _____

Enumeration District _____ Date of Enumeration _____ Enumerator _____ Publication No. _____ Reel No. _____

House No.	Dwelling No.	Family No.	Name of person whose abode on April 15 was with this family. Children born after, omitted.	Relationship to head of family	Sex	Color/Race	Age	Marital Status	Years married	Mother of how many children	No. of these children living	Person's birthplace	Father's birthplace	Mother's birthplace	Year of immigration	Naturalized/Alien	English/Language	Occupation	Industry Establishment	Emp/W/OA	Employee out of work: April 15, 1910	Employee out of work: Weeks during 1909	Education: Read	Education: Write	Education: School since Sep. 1, 1909	Home Ownership: Owned/Rented	Home Ownership: Free of mortgage	Home Ownership: Farm/House	Home Ownership: Schedule Number	U-C Vet. Army/Navy	Blind both eyes	Deaf and Dumb

Form 14

EXTRACT FROM 1910 CENSUS

Extract by _____

State _____ County or Parish _____ Township, Ward or Beat _____ Incorporated Place _____

Enumeration District _____ Date of Enumeration _____ Enumerator _____ Publication No. _____ Reel No. _____

House No.	Dwelling No.	Family No.	Name of person whose abode on April 15 was with this family. Children born after, omitted.	Relationship to head of family	Sex	Color/Race	Age	Marital Status	Years married	Mother of how many children	No. of these children living	Person's birthplace	Father's birthplace	Mother's birthplace	Year of immigration	Naturalized/Alien	English/Language	Occupation	Industry Establishment	Emp/W/OA	April 15, 1910	Weeks during 1909	Read	Write	School since Sep. 1, 1909	Owned/Rented	Free of mortgage	Farm/House	Schedule Number	U-C Vet. Army/Navy	Blind both eyes	Deaf and Dumb

Form 14

EXTRACT FROM 1910 CENSUS

Extract by _____

State _____ County or Parish _____ Township, Ward or Beat _____ Incorporated Place _____

Enumeration District _____ Date of Enumeration _____ Enumerator _____ Publication No. _____ Reel No. _____

House No.	Dwelling No.	Family No.	Name of person whose abode on April 15 was with this family. Children born after, omitted.	Relationship to head of family	Sex	Color/Race	Age	Marital Status	Years married	Mother of how many children	No. of these children living	Person's birthplace	Father's birthplace	Mother's birthplace	Year of immigration	Naturalized/Alien	English/Language	Occupation	Industry Establishment	Emp/W/OA	April 15, 1910	Weeks during 1909	Read	Write	School since Sep. 1, 1909	Owned/Rented	Free of mortgage	Farm/House	Schedule Number	U-C	Vet. Army/Navy	Blind both eyes	Deaf and Dumb

Form 14

EXTRACT FROM 1910 CENSUS

Extract by _____

State _____ County or Parish _____ Township, Ward or Beat _____ Incorporated Place _____

Enumeration District _____ Date of Enumeration _____ Enumerator _____ Publication No. _____ Reel No. _____

House No.	Dwelling No.	Family No.	Name of person whose abode on April 15 was with this family. Children born after, omitted.	Relationship to head of family	Sex	Color/Race	Age	Marital Status	Years married	Mother of how many children	No. of these children living	Person's birthplace	Father's birthplace	Mother's birthplace	Year of immigration	Naturalized/Alien	English/ Language	Occupation	Industry Establishment	Emp/W/OA	April 15, 1910	Weeks during 1909	Read	Write	School since Sep. 1, 1909	Owned/ Rented	Free of mortgage	Farm/ House	Schedule Number	U-C Vet. Army/Navy	Blind both eyes	Deaf and Dumb

Employee out of work: April 15, 1910 / Weeks during 1909
Education: Read / Write / School since Sep. 1, 1909
Home Ownership: Owned/Rented / Free of mortgage / Farm/House / Schedule Number

Form 14